FROGS DON'T SING RED

FROGS DON'T SING RED

Poems

by Sandi Stromberg

© 2023 Sandi Stromberg. All rights reserved.
This material may not be reproduced in any form, published,
reprinted, recorded, performed, broadcast,
rewritten or redistributed without
the explicit permission of Sandi Stromberg.
All such actions are strictly prohibited by law.

Cover design by Shay Culligan
Cover photo by kai brune on unsplash
Author photo by Wyatt McSpadden

Library of Congress Control Number: 2023935743

ISBN: 978-1-63980-316-3

Kelsay Books
502 South 1040 East, A-119
American Fork, Utah 84003
Kelsaybooks.com

In memory of Bill Turner (1939–2021)
who brought poetry into my life

For my sons, my daughters-in-law, my grandsons
Erik, Melissa, and Alex
Dirk, Sheryl, and Johan

For Ron Schenk
who reminds me that life is a poetic adventure

Art is the burning bush that both shelters and makes visible our profounder longings.
—Art [Objects] by Jeanette Winterson

Acknowledgments

With gratitude to the editors and publications in which these poems originally appeared, sometimes in a slightly different form.

Brabant Cultureel (in Dutch and English): "'s maandags rond het middaguur," "Mondays at Noon"

Chaos Dive Reunion Anthology: "This Is a Valentine"

Colere: A Journal of Cultural Exploration: "Mondays at Noon," "The Dutch Class"

easing the edges: a collection of everyday miracles: "A Day on Tinos"

ENOUGH, Finalist, Public Poetry Annual International Competition: "The Pianist's Gift"

Equinox: "After a Day's Sail on the North Sea"

Illya's Honey: "Frogs Don't Sing Red," "Shelter"

Houston Poetry Fest Anthology: "Beyondness," "Fourteen Kinds of Loneliness," "The Art Asylum," "The Women Come and Go," "There Are Reasons"

Improbable Worlds: "October"

Medium Digest: "Forecast"

MockingHeart Review: "Sunrise Walk in the Heights," "Widow's Diptych or Now That My Husband's Gone"

Ocotillo Review: "I Saw My First Egret Walking the Ditch Through the Smoke of Rice Fields Burning"

Panoply, A Literary Zine: "Once Upon a Threshold"

Purifying Wind: "To Believe in Angels and Demons"

San Pedro River Review: "*Herenhuis:* Homage to My Dutch Home"

Starry, Starry Night Ekphrastic Anthology inspired by Van Gogh's Masterpiece: "I Ask Van Gogh's *Starry Night* to Forgive Me"

Still the Waves Beat: "A Distant Mirror"

Texas Poetry Calendars: "Lake Buchanan Sanctuary," "Leaving Comfort, Texas on FM 473," "Sycamore Dreams"

The Ekphrastic Review: "A Distant Mirror," "A Glass of Muscadet," "A Path Home," "Checkered Floor," "dear sea sprites," "Derangement," "Did Psyche and Eros Know?" "In a Galaxy Not Far Away," "In the Land of Shadow Puppets," "Make No Mistake," "Nevermore Forever," "Our Earthly Lot," "Psyche Has a Word with the Poet," "Robbery at the Musée Magritte," "Shadowy Assemblage," "Suspending the Surreal," "The Mermaid and Slavic Soul," "Through the Keyhole," "To Cultivate a Garden," "When a Voice Was All I Had"

The Orchards Poetry Journal: "Ecru Silk and the Ormolu Clock"

Unknotting the Line: The Poetry in Prose: "Prescription for Widowhood"

Waco WordFest Anthology—AIR: "Aerie"

Weaving the Terrain: 100-Word Southwestern Poems: "A Li Po Moment in West Texas"

Windows—An Anthology: "Daydreaming"

Words Become Shadows as Our Spirits Rise: "Make No Mistake"

Special Thanks

To Lorette C. Luzajic, founder and editor of *The Ekphrastic Review,* for the gifts she brings to writers through her publication and personal touch. Her friendship and encouragement have enhanced my writing and life.

To Tina Carlson and John Milkereit, who voluntarily brought their talents and encouragement to make this collection what it is.

To the dynamic duo, Scott Wiggerman and David Meischen. Both extraordinary teachers and writers. Weeklong workshops with Scott in the Big Bend area of Texas brought new focus. Workshops with David brought me through the pandemic and gave me poetic space to process grief and bring these poems together.

To those whose feedback along the way has made a significant difference in my poetic life as well as these poems: Stan Crawford, Margo Davis, Priscilla Frake, Cindy Huyser, Sharon Klander, Gabrielle Langley, Gayle Lauradunn, Eileen Lawrence, Varsha Saraiya-Shah, and Rebecca Spears.

Contents

Frogs Don't Sing Red   17

Wrapped in My Own Desert

There Are Reasons   21
Shelter   22
A Distant Mirror   23
The Art Asylum   25
The Women Come and Go   27
Nightshade   28
To Cultivate a Garden   29
To Believe in Angels and Demons   30
Section 27, Grave #66   31
Our Earthly Lot   32

Dew of the Sea

Shadowy Assemblage   35
Once Upon a Threshold   36
Sycamore Dreams   37
A Day on Tinos   38
Once in the Blue Ridge Mountains   39
Make No Mistake   40
The Dutch Class in North Brabant   41
After a Day's Sail on the North Sea   42
Herenhuis: Homage to My Dutch Home   43
Mondays at Noon   45
Suspending the Surreal   46

Moments of Prayer

I Saw My First Egret Walking the Ditch
    Through the Smoke of Rice Fields Burning   49
Checkered Floor   50
Fourteen Kinds of Loneliness   51

The Mermaid and Slavic Soul	52
October	53
Lake Buchanan Sanctuary	54
Leaving Comfort, Texas on FM 473	55
A Li Po Moment in West Texas	56
The Pianist's Gift	57
dear sea sprites	58

Circling Then Moving Deep

Daydreaming	61
Ecru Silk and the Ormolu Clock	62
Forecast	63
He Told Her It Wasn't a Date, She Had to Take Him to Dinner	64
Did Psyche and Eros Know?	65
Derangement	67
Robbery at the Musée Magritte	68
Beyondness	69
When a Voice Was All I Had	70
Buy That Red Dress	71
In a French Café	72
A Path Home	73
Aerie	74
Sunrise Walk in the Heights	75
No Visitors Allowed	76

A Dream to Pierce the Dark

I Ask Van Gogh's *Starry Night* to Forgive Me	79
Nevermore Forever	80
Grief Has Its Habits	81
In the Land of Shadow Puppets	83
Through the Keyhole	84
Tankas: All the Tomorrows	85

Widow's Diptych
    or Now That My Husband's Gone   86
This Is a Valentine   88
A Glass of Muscadet   90
Psyche Has a Word with the Poet   91
In a Galaxy Not Far Away   92
Prescription for Widowhood   93

Frogs Don't Sing Red

Les grenouilles ne chantent pas rouge by Max Ernst

I can't find amphibians
in the bone-like fibers

twisted on red canvas in a red
room, but I can hear their song

across a lazy pond, a jasmine-scented
memory, waiting for the breeze

to play its melody through still
leaves. A quiet, punctuated

by green-throbbing throats and
fireflies, the cries of children's

hide and seek, while I nestle,
a silkworm spinning threads

under the mulberry tree
on the night-damp ground.

Wrapped in My Own Desert

There Are Reasons

Please excuse my mother   *lamentations*
vicissitudes martyrdom   I came without

operating instructions. My birth drained her
last thousand dollars, the war just over.

And my father   *duty lethargy*
denial   born to ramble, dreams trapped

in black-and-white tv. His life focused
on flittering images, days of disappointed teaching.

Please excuse their parenting   *inept conflicted*
Bible-thumping   they'd none

themselves orphaned as teenagers, shocked
at a baby's reality.

See the humanity in them   *struggle poverty*
mistakes   no one gets to practice.

Shelter

After my friend's father dies—her mother
long since gone—we stand together in
an art gallery, a co-op of uneven
talents. She says she's lost
the family umbrella. I picture her
drenched, unprotected, and think of
the black and white triangles, the wide
circumference of my own shelter,
its steel-rod spine. So different
from my childhood's weak stem,
flimsy ribs bent back by fickle gusts,
one section ripped and billowing.
Mine was leaky, I say. A wan smile
passes across her lips. *Oh, yes,
mine, too, but aren't they all?*
Half femme fatale, half lost waif,
she turns toward a collage of eyes
cut from magazines, their myriad
colors and slants a whole life's
journey from surprised discovery to
middle-aged resignation to inconsolable
grief and, finally, back to wonder.

A Distant Mirror

The Chess Game by Sofonisba Anguissola

My sisters and I have played chess for years,
sharpening our skills and sometimes
our nails. We are good at making
unpredictable moves, drawing

a little blood, carving a few scars.
Yet, forever sisters, delivered
from the same womb, we are bound by
our mother's blood and body.

On her 95th birthday, we call
a truce, lay down our pawns and bishops,
knights and castles, a lifetime of skirmishes
and jealousies to gather photos, banners,

coffee, lemonade—then order
a half-chocolate-half-vanilla cake,
butter-creamed with yellow roses
for the Texas-born queen. Outside, severe winds

and rain whip around the city, the house,
an echo of our tornado-prone
history. But our perennial game design,
as we crisscross the board, has always been

to retain a sweet, sisterly image,
good manners, deceptive smiles. *The Chess Game*
reveals a pecking order. Europa gives
her older sister a charming,

yet mischievous smile. Hand raised, Minerva
concedes checkmate to *her* older sister.
And Lucia looks directly
at the artist who paints expressions

that might tell other stories, ones that only
the old servant, watching intently from the side,
could tell us—as I hint at ours now.

The Art Asylum

A depository of life's paraphernalia

i.

When I hear about this harbor for life's
miscellany, a safe house for the discarded,

I am dragging home boxes of mementoes
from my office. Keeper or kitsch? Each item begs

for existence in my overstuffed study.
An angel's annunciation to Mary

painted on glass, a wooden Statue
of Liberty, a plastic Buddha,

a dancing porcelain hippo,
all those dedicated years.

ii.

My Depression-raised mother sits
in her apartment, smothered. Loss,

a river of pain. Her closet doors
won't shut on dresses and jackets

she has owned for forty years.
Eight decades of clippings wait to be read.

Impatiens, amaryllis, and others whose names
I do not know crowd every corner.

Among her prizes, she caresses the quilt
she won at the family reunion in 1954.

It is then I know I cannot be
the sanctuary for my every treasure.

The Art Asylum appears as my *deus ex machina*.
Salvation, a warehouse god.

The Women Come and Go

My friend signs her e-mail

Sweet violets, Lee,
instead of *Cheers* or *Love.*

She knows the downside of a kitchen knife,
the problems it won't solve. She has seen it

in Viv Eliot, who married into the waste land,
the tyranny of rogue hormones.

Does this Lee who appears on my Facebook feed
know about my grandmother, too?

About her epilepsy and rage and the stages
of a woman's life? About screaming murder

into the night, sobbing into the morning?
The violence of slingshot emotions

that injure the innocent? I falter here, fearful
of this inheritance and how estrogen

links her to me across the half century
since she sat, finally calm and deliberate,

on the front porch, rocking memories.
At moments, I've stood on her edge, tried

the flat world of drugs, experienced
the betrayal of hollow men

then stepped back
to hear the music of gypsy violins.

Nightshade

In my sleep, I crossed
the English Channel in a two-prop
plane, flew over waters as dark

as my childhood. Both my baggage
and mother abandoned in Paris.
For once, I traveled light, no excess to pay.

My body drifted like a helium balloon
toward a new shore. I thought of
the plane's contrail, an umbilical

evaporating as dawn started
her purple-rose conquest. The glowing sky
full of pastel promise, possibility.

I swooped over chalk cliffs.
Green fields and downs undulated.
The landing smooth. At customs, a tingling

raced through my nerves. I'd arrived
on the other side of the separating water,
moved into the terminal—my own woman.

It was then I saw my mother waiting
on the other side of the sun-sparkled glass.
Or was it, after all, only my reflection?

To Cultivate a Garden

"All I know," said Candide, "is that we must cultivate our garden."
—Voltaire

Every week, the stained-glass windows of my father's first church
cast their deep reds and blues across the faces
of both the young and the aging, his assigned plot
of congregants. Fifteen on a good Sunday in this town
of 400. Fern Rogers opened each service, striking
the piano keys slowly and with emphasis, as though
fast motion would break the sacred spell of her religious fervor.
She closed with "Just As I Am, I Come,"
at a pace ample for a procession of hundreds, though hardly
anyone came to dedicate a life to God. Participants were either
too young, their parents having dropped them off
and gone for coffee at the only café, or too old
and already secure in their salvation on Judgment Day. But
for several seasons my father persevered like any gardener
who knows there will be good years and lean ones.

To Believe in Angels and Demons

The Isenheim Altarpiece, Colmar, France

We travel by plane, train, and foot.
A sort of pilgrimage to a medieval Christ,
his pocked body hung on Grünewald's cross,
suffering for our red and painful sins. Heresy
well meant—a diseased Jesus giving succor
to the sick and dying.

      From a side panel, St. Anthony's temptation
casts its fierce shadow over me. His plight
in the desert echoing the drone
of childhood's Sunday sermons.
Hellfire and damnation, brimstone
and blood. I brewed my own
draughts of fear. My familiars—a bestiary
writhing with reptiles and vultures, ferocious
claws and forked tongues. In our closets
and under my bed. Their punishing
spirits flashing through the house,
demons on the loose.

      At night, I curled into myself
for warmth against their chilling grasp.
My thoughts on the smooth brow
of our dining room Jesus. His wavy
brown beard and deep-blue robe,
his pale white face in profile as he
looked toward what I knew must be
heaven, the safeguard of angels.

      Oh, how quickly childhood
images manifest! I stand transfixed, silent
and alone before St. Anthony, wrapped,
like contemplatives before me,
in my own desert. A long-buried shiver
slithers up my spine.

Section 27, Grave #66

Veterans Memorial Cemetery, Fayetteville, Arkansas

White crosses curve
across August's green
hillside, weathered soldiers
waiting for inspection.

Twelve guns crack
still air, burst through
thin walls we've built
around our loss.

Four khaki-clad men
snap stars and stripes,
turn red and white
in perfect triangles,
each tight fold

holding my father.

Our Earthly Lot

El Purgatorio by Cristóbal Rojas

Just when you hope to lead the perfect,
    sinless life, here comes Purgatory again.
        A reminder. The blazing flame

of the seventh circle meant to cleanse, but
    in the moment agonizing. Raised
        in the church, you still endure fear and trembling,

relive the traumas of childhood. You know
    the poison ivy of disobedience,
        the fiery itch that cannot be relieved,

the threat of 500 years of suffering
    to erase traces of misdoing.
        The misery of the dispossessed,

the sick and despairing,
    the victims of social injustice—
        purgatory on Earth.

You know that lot. Cristóbal Rojas
    painted what he himself
        understood then carried

El Purgatorio home with him.
    From Paris to Caracas and
        the Iglesia de La Davina Pastora.

His consumptive body center-stage
    in the dramatic conflagration
        as other shades walk through its flames

seeking release. An angel hovers above.
    If only we could trust
        in the promise of Heaven.

Dew of the Sea

Shadowy Assemblage

Pharmacy, a Joseph Cornell shadow box, 1942

They appear innocent
enough, these clear glass bottles,
uniform, filled with random discoveries
from souvenir stalls, thrift shops,
flea markets, trash cans. Who can say
what this debris was before?

Meaningless? Dangerous?
Best left untouched?
Under the box, it says *Pharmacy.*
If I lift the glass stoppers, what
might I unleash into the world?
Pandora's chaotic assortment

of the world's maladies or
my shadow? Maybe that coiled shell,
second shelf middle, holds
my anger, unacknowledged
and hidden like a hermit crab
deep inside its spiral. Maybe

the black beans and fire-red pepper,
bottom shelf middle, hide my hot,
unlived sauciness. Maybe each particle
in the bottle, top shelf far left, the one
whose intense indigo first caught
my eye holds every blue hour,

blue dream, blue feeling
crowding my life, dragging me down
into sad song one minute,
donning light the next.

Once Upon a Threshold

It's a new dawn.
—Jefferson Airplane

Decades have passed since I stepped over
      the threshold of Bois-Gentil, the spring
           of those butterfly movements in my womb.

Geneva's gray lifted as alpine peaks
      sloughed off winter's pea-soup. Glaciers sparkled
           like white quartz against deep blue.

And I entered the clinic, its palatial Swiss elegance
      devoted to birth. Contractions quickening,
           I barely noticed the dark green shutters

and red-tiled roof. It's only now, from a photo
      found deep in the web's Swiss history, that I see
           their vividness against a graceful white façade.

That I learn the fate of the Clinic "Kind Wood,"
      scene of my rite of passage into motherhood.
           A ghost of my past, it no longer sits amidst

perfumed gardens on the route de Malagnou.
      Yet, the odor of roses, white and purple lilacs,
           and flowers whose names I never knew

still waft through my mind's French doors—
      no longer stalled in winter bleakness,
           waiting for life to start.

Sycamore Dreams

Country music two-steps around a worn
leather couch. Flickers of yellow and orange
rise from smoldering logs. And my pen glides
across the lined page, gathering thoughts.
Outside, drizzle fogs the air. Ice crystals
drop from leaf tips onto the redwood deck,
tinkling as clear and crystalline
as a triangle.
                       All is so right
with my world, I would stop time in the middle
of this moment, snuggle into an endless
winter. But when the flames fall
into their embers, and the ice crystals melt,
my blood rushes on.
                       I anticipate—
the way the sycamore dreams of spring buds
or the stag, drinking at the creek, aspires
to more points on his antlers. The way
I hold my breath, a mother watching
my sons' lives unfold, step by step.

A Day on Tinos

How can I explain the softness
    of prickly rosemary?
        The warmth that floods me

as the Greek driver jumps
    from the taxi, picks a bouquet of branches,
        then lays them in my unexpecting arms?

For the mother of two blond, blue-eyed boys,
    his dark eyes seem to say, his tongue
        not knowing the English words.

With a deep bow, he drapes me
    in rosemary, the "dew of the sea,"
        like Aphrodite when she rose

from the Aegean. Here on Tinos' gray-brown hills
    high above the water, his gift awakens
        a thirst to be seen, sustenance

for those long spells of drought. In the flicker
    of dreams, I learn to gather
        its wild scent for remembrance.

Once in the Blue Ridge Mountains

With a line from Larry Levis

There are places where the eye can starve,
but not in Virginia with its ridge
of blue-tinged mountains. Here, for example,
was a townhouse where our family lived
with walls of windows. A view
that invited itself into our lives.
A view that said, "Blue lives here, too,"
although the walls were white
and the tiled floors white. Valleys
undulated below the slope of the house
before the land rose again. The forest between
was thick enough to hide houses and people
so that we thought
all of this was just for us
and every night at bedtime,
though we didn't know it yet,
Sorrow climbed the stairs with us. It slept
in the guest room, sometimes appeared
at the dinner table. Uninvited. Though there was
an odd word or glance that started to sneak in.
You know how the past tense turns a sentence dark.
On a winter day, I stood with the view
and pulled back the white lace curtains
with their delicate pattern of evergreens,
outlining the bluish trees beyond.
And I thought something that I already knew
in my body: all was not well. The in-laws arrived
for a visit. The pipes froze
and burst, flooding the house.
The builders had gotten it all wrong.
But none of that matters now.

Make No Mistake

The Domino Players by Horace Pippin

We play dominoes on an old card table
my husband has carried into the garden.
A summer afternoon in Amish Lancaster County,

a box of black tiles, three generations together
in Pennsylvania's sedate green hills.
Until now, you may think, dear reader,

that a family board game with pips and tiles
would be harmonious. But no more so
than this painting of domino players.

Let's not mistake either scene for domestic bliss.
My father-in-law's stroke does not inhibit
his wily draw of black tiles, their white pips hidden

as he builds a battle wall. He's foxy,
competitive, grumpy. When asked how he is,
he always claims, "mean and miserable."

His scowl a perfect poker-face not unlike
Pippin's matriarch in her blue shawl and
scarlet headdress. Look closely at the sharp,

open scissors lying on the blood-red cloth,
the flame-red teeth in the coal fire, the red tongues
of the oil lamps. Take care when adding

a tile to the line as it marches across the table.
And when no tiles in your pile fit the strip,
beware a trip to the boneyard.

The Dutch Class in North Brabant

We travel from opposite directions
to this ammonia-scrubbed Tower
of Babel. Scratched tables and
blackboards grown gray with age.

I come from the West. My life tidy,
predictable, safe. They arrive
from points East: Iraq, Iran, Kurdistan,
Palestine, and Herzegovina.

Places where borders bump
each other and centuries-old feuds
won't die, from countries where the price
of saying what they think is greater

than pocket change.
For me, freedom of speech
is a loaf of bread, but for them,
she's a seducer whose lure

they followed to a promised land.
Their opinions loosened from strangleholds,
they argue passionately in this language
I cannot wrap my tongue around.

They understand sentences,
the splitting of words and how verbs,
those symbols of action,
are always hidden until the end.

After a Day's Sail on the North Sea

Colijnsplaat, Netherlands

That was the year my ring finger twisted
in the shackle of my marriage.

Sunday afternoon's parade of sailboats
single-filed into the marina. My husband

motoring too fast, I jumped onto the pier,
the last hope between dock and nine-ton boat.

When the engine stilled, water softly lapped
the wooden planks. I tore my finger loose

from between boat and stanchion. My sons,
shocked and helpless, followed their father's order,

"Take care of your mom." Seagulls swooped above,
mewing while my husband closed the boat.

Waves beat at the hull making it shiver
as blood gushed down my hand. Overhead,

the rigging chimed and clanked against the mast.
And now I ask why, after a village doctor

stitched the fingertip back on, I went home and cooked
dinner for my family? When was it I lost my mooring?

Herenhuis: Homage to My Dutch Home

> *The houses I had they took away from me.*
> —George Seferis

Three words scrolled across the lintel
above the green-lacquered door—*Het Wit Anker,*
The White Anchor.

           As though a name
were a promise, I dropped my own anchor,
lowered hook-shaped hopes toward what I wanted,

a safe harbor. An end to my life's
endless gyre. The cold Dutch spring was colored
with tulips

           and brisk winds under a gray,
lowering sky. Handmade lace with graceful swans
curtained my windows. Market town sounds

became symphonic. The cathedral carillon,
quarter-hour chimes and bicycle bells, buses
rumbling cobblestones,

           all-night revelries
during the town's own *Carnaval* until *Dikke Dinsdag*
Mardi Gras. Seasons and years passed.

Neighbors chatted and chastised in the throaty
weight of Dutch—my stoop too sooty, windows
too rain streaked.

           Once, a man rapped at my door,
wanting to tell me he was born in my attic,
then tipped his hat and moved on down the street.

That last spring, the flowering almond whose branches
tapped the kitchen's leaded-pane window died.
Icy storms blew inland

                              from the North Sea,
tore at the anchor and threw me off course.

Mondays at Noon

The carillon still plays in my mind
most Mondays at noon. Two dozen years,
thousands of miles ago, stuck

like a needle on vinyl, playing Bach
and the Beatles, Bach and the Beatles.
Notes chime over images I hoard,

from the pepper-shaker steeple
of Sint-Gertrudiskerk, up the Hoogstraat,
over the cobblestones, around the gentle curve

to what was once my gabled house.
How could I think I would live out
my days in that village with its frites

and shawarma, strong coffee, and guttural
Dutch? The music cuts double-edged—
memory's bane and balm—as I sit

across the Atlantic in my craftsman cottage.
No church bells toll the quarter hours
in the humid South, relentless sunny days

instead of the warm wrap of the North Sea's
low, gray sky. Each recalled note lifts,
lonely as a loon's call across the ocean.

Suspending the Surreal

Tickets are cheap at the Potato Theatre.
The stage, dark as a moonless midnight.

The plot, indecipherable as Linear B
(used to be). The actors as inscrutable

as Buddhas. A moth clings to a wooden pier,
rotting before my eyes, and I suspend

disbelief. A familiar dread conjures up
my dreamer's dark tangle of personalities.

Am I caterpillar, dangling on the branch
of a sunken tree, or the transformed moth?

Perhaps the white-faced Pierrot
with androgynous expression—

sad, soft, almost tender—for the blue and green
bodies, each rising on a leg as sturdy

as a telephone pole. Or are we a three-handed,
two-legged chimera, shape-shifted,

commanding stage left. Behind us,
whitewashed buildings call out Home. Home.

How tempted I am to swim out to them
before they sink into the theatre's darkness

where, the sole member of the audience,
I am trapped in inescapable images.

Moments of Prayer

I Saw My First Egret Walking the Ditch
Through the Smoke of Rice Fields Burning

Forget what I say about the chinch bugs and the fire ants.
The hole punched in the bathroom wall.
I took solace with the solitary egret.
The address, Redwood Bend Trail held the first three lies.
The game room sheltered a model railroad.
There were dreams I can't remember of a train.
The master bedroom oozed luxury, walk-in closet,
bathroom with bubbling Jacuzzi.
Fire ants struggled for pantry primacy.
I stopped reading the paper, listening to the news.
The day my husband lost his job, we picnicked
in the garden while the back door locked us out.
Chinch bugs chewed up St. Augustine's grass.
Someone's fist smashed the car window.
The air-conditioner came to a metal-crunching halt.
My husband U-Hauled himself out the drive.
The egret moved to another ditch.

Checkered Floor

Checkered Floor by Leah Gose

At Thanksgiving, I sort twenty-five years
of marriage, lay the photos in piles,
label them according to place.
        The nuclear fallout is unexpected.
I avoid the table, learn to walk
around it, looking away from our faces,
the seventeen nests I'd built. The twigs and
wattle of townhouses, apartments,
the London flat, the wing of a manor house.
        Finally, a detached, single-family home
where none of the pieces fit,
like this photo
        of a torn photo
                of a room.
Its floor of checkered tiles—alternating black
and white—though a divorce is never without
some gray. The splintered walls shorn,
wallpaper stripped, baseboards whose joints
no longer meet.
        Why do I want to lift the photo
from the frame and take it home? Even if I place
the pieces where I used to think they belonged,
the edges will always be jagged.

Fourteen Kinds of Loneliness

i.

Sentries stood for centuries along China's Great Wall,
quietly awaiting Mongolians. From aeries higher than
eagles' nests they lived the lonely truth of Chinese
paintings, the ones with steep gray mountains plunging
to valleys, a red bird poised on green bamboo.

ii.

A photographer rents a Scottish croft, focuses his lens
on the lone sheep outside his window. Miles
from the next farm, he writes that she watches him
as much as he watches her.

iii.

This evening, a rustle breaks the Hill Country stillness
where I contemplate mesquite and roll a poet's words
about loneliness around in my fingers.
I turn to eyes locked on mine. Seven deer.
I freeze, as intent on them
as they on me, wanting them to stay.

The Mermaid and Slavic Soul

In *Gogol's Dream,* I would be
the mermaid, as I once was.

Sheathed in silver foil, my legs
undulating to synchronized music.

Again and again, I dove and surfaced,
fettered. But in this painting,

I feel free, pressing a lotus
to my left breast, my purity cradled

in a white canoe, clean and fragrant.
Gogol holds his heart—reverent, aching

with Russian soul—ready to pluck
and offer it as the blossom of his love.

A troika and three curious horses stand
stalwart behind him. In another instant,

I know he will take my hand, abandon
his surreal, satiric pen that birthed

The Nose (his self-consciousness about
his own) and *The Overcoat.* Together,

we will remain poised on the fertile plain
of Ukraine, banked by windmill, village,

dacha, and cushioned in the pastel
softness of the unconscious.

October

Early morning air, thinning. Light
at a different slant. Sycamore leaves
and bark filling the driveway and deck.
Pesky squirrels hide and seek through
hollows in the live oak, dig
in my flowerpots. Pecans and acorns,
still green and sour, disappearing
beneath their claws. Geraniums
uprooted. A lazy breeze whispers to
swaying leaves. Each slight rustle
loosening their stronghold. Their falling
a silent death. A wood thrush knocks
at my window, demanding entry.
Its brown-speckled breast
throbbing at each thrust. Through memory's door
wafts Mother's homemade chili sauce with
its vinegar breath. Me with Asian flu. My first
glimpse of alpine snows covering autumn's
brittle yellows, reds, and browns.
It's the early twilight.
It's the faith of squirrels.
It's the persistence of the thrush.
It's all Octobers, dappling my mind
with golden flecks as sunlight weakens.

Lake Buchanan Sanctuary

On the hillside above deep fried and barbeque,
Mariah serves organic, sprouted grain and seeds,
fresh-fruit smoothies, fish. She's hooked

on Paleo cuisine, Spanish guitar, her notions
of spirituality.
              In the guest book, I read

how she and her husband, now dead, built
this community of cottages and sheds
below a hilltop sanctuary where the spirits

often come. She looks askance at me and says,
"You have to be receptive." And she's right. I'm
probably not.
           I've seen too much damage

in the name of spiritual intent. Even so I sit
in the stone circle amidst pungent junipers, deep
purple blossoms, my eyes closed in anticipation.

Is doubt a deterrent? I dismiss the thought and
concentrate on the slight breeze tinkling a bevy
              of chimes. Their pitches in and out

of sync, they blend point and counterpoint. I meditate,
relax my mind, breathe deeply. As I indulge
in the soft blend of birdsong and chime,

a slight ruffle moves against cheek. Eyes
shoot open. Flashes of yellow, orange, and blue
flit silently. Butterflies.
          Their shadows traversing numinous ground.

Leaving Comfort, Texas on FM 473

Young, lithe, lovely, she races
down the farm-to-market road,
dodging my car, searching
for courage. The buck she runs with
carries a rack of antlers that mark him
seasons older. But age makes no difference
to this young doe. With the elegant grace
of a ballet dancer, he leaps the six-foot,
barbed-wire fence and pauses in the field,
turning his head toward her as they begin
a parallel course. His eyes command,
"Jump. Jump. Now. Now."
And I think of my own fears of leaping
as I pull to the side of the road.
The doe charges the barrier. Each time,
when her young legs refuse to leap, my blood
leaps for them, my breath held as she halts,
lowers her head in what seems a moment
of prayer, or perhaps the prayer is mine.

A Li Po Moment in West Texas

From my perch in the Creek House,
lace cactus, stubborn sycamores, ball moss

looped like earrings over branches of live oak.
Centuries-old cypress dip spindly legs

into the water. Seven deer hightail the fence.
Why the red-throated buzzard above?

Last night, the sky split open
its gray-cloud promise, thunderous music

on my tin roof. Today, sunlight filters
through heavy raindrops, a dewy web woven

between limbs. *Come, drink,* the spider invites.
I linger in this wicker chair, a chittering squirrel

questioning my presence, and wish for a blue
butterfly, etched in black, to alight on my hand.

The Pianist's Gift

Für Elise awakens the heart, stretches
across the keyboard, reaches the child in me.

For two nights my dreams found me sleeping
in the hull of a sunflower seed, grown large

enough to fit my body—a cradle, a cage,
a berth for pain? Who can say when

one truly sleeps? Last night my back burdened,
the left knee's burn, children birthed and grown away.

The piano's fingers caress this bagatelle
cocooned for forty years after Beethoven's

death. My heart bids me carry its notes
out of the concert hall on a small, satin

pillow—like a pageboy carries down the aisle.
To make tonight's hull plush enough

to conceive a dream with tender melancholy.

dear sea sprites

Sea Sprites in Flight by John Anster Fitzgerald

i weave myself into the waves of your fantasy
a reverie unspoiled by the dull world i live in

i want a pair of diaphanous dragonfly wings
the wispy shimmer of their red purple green

the ability to take flights when i fancy
in an unbounded universe

to have friends like these luminous fairies
wrapped in stars

how one grows wings
how to find the secret shores

hear the answers whispered on the wind

Circling Then Moving Deep

Daydreaming

If I were a window, I could frame a world
of possibilities, make them as crisp

as an architect's blueprint. One colorful pane intersecting
another, my overwhelms calmed in the formality

of black or cleansed by the magic of purple. On rainy days
I could gaze out over red-tiled roofs splashed

with blue. On cautious days I could hide my face
behind soft peach. If I were a window, I could be

opaque. Passersby would see only shadows, my dark
moods projected on a flickering screen. Or I could

take a risk, be transparent, let each day unfold in colors
as bold as a peacock—the sky filled with the royal blue

of awakening—or find rest in the powdery tones
of a fountain's soft trickle. Such peace, stability. If the day

dawned green, I could watch a meadow, listen
to the deep throats of cow bells, fill with well-being.

If a window, I could welcome fiery red days—
danger, passion, anger, romance. As each night fell,

the colors would darken, then transform into deeper hues,
a velvet carpet dotted with the Milky Way.

Ecru Silk and the Ormolu Clock

Hôtel Argouges, Bayeux, France

for Melissa

Magical emptiness greets me this morning—
the breakfast room all mine. My rickety sense
of sophistication in France not yet endangered.

I feign a certain elegance as I sweep toward
a window table and its Louis XVI chair, the style
fancied by Marie-Antoinette.

As though I, too, were born to live this way,
I lean into its medallion-shaped back,
run my ringed fingers over the ecru silk

and breathe the aroma of fresh ground
Arabica beans. A cold March arches its frosty light
through high, paned windows, starching tablecloths

white, and falls on an enclosed garden
revealing the tight buds of spring. Past centuries
harmonize with the nine o'clock chime

of the ormolu clock in this fairy tale palace.
No matter that in bygone days, women like me
were servants, never clothed in crinoline and brocade.

I gather my *petit dejeuner,* spread butter on dark slices
of baguette, threaded with sesame seeds and hazelnuts

and sip my *café au lait*. Deliciously alone
in this communion, I savor *once upon a time.*

Forecast

When he stands before my desk, I look
past him, tempted as I eye my umbrella.

A storm brews outside these windows,
but it's hard to know if love will come.

Its appearance is as unpredictable
as scattered showers, and perhaps I prefer

a long dry spell to frenetic activity,
the twenty questions it pelts at my heart,

the ones my mind thinks should be answered.
I watch clouds accumulate and darken

but I'm clear. I don't want
a flashy cloudburst. I would exchange

late summer monsoons for the soft sound
of drops on the roof and the smell of spring.

He Told Her It Wasn't a Date,
She Had to Take Him to Dinner

He pressed a solid crease

        in his grey wool trousers,

    polished his Bass loafers.

She planted yellow-faced pansies on her balcony.

      Autumn had arrived and along with it

the season of performing arts.

        They met at the ballet.

    Expectant. A shiver

of risk as their eyes locked

        across the lobby.

Side by side for the first time,

    they shared

        Franz Lehár's *The Merry Widow*.

Later, at the little bistro, she fed him

    oysters *daemon*.

Did Psyche and Eros Know?

Lovers in Small Boat (The Demon Lover) by Maximilian Pirner

i.

An erotic link,
the neck,
head to torso
sympathetic nerve
begging touch.
She braces,
leaning across his leg
clutching her innocence
in white lace against
the boat's wooden side.
Water that alchemists,
could turn into wine.
Kisses lure and release
her to him,
seduced beyond
questioning
his intentions.

ii.

Our third date,
cars illegally parked
side by side. We stood
in the dripping heat, caressed
by humidity. Middle-aged,
divorced, children grown. And he did
what I wanted.

I hadn't told him. I hadn't known
what was missing from the lost
marriage until I saw
the made-for-tv-movie. The film's

slow motion, like foreplay. The actor
cherishing the woman before him,
an unexpected move
that made me hunger.

As we moved toward each other,
my lover-to-be dropped
his keys to the ground and embraced
my face. Inched
his fingers down my neck
circling it then moving
deep into the dark brown
thickness of my hair and drew me
to his lips.

Derangement

Frenzy by Władysław Podkowiński

I am Zeus of the darkness
red of eye
rabid with lust

she is no Godiva
her raving red mane doesn't
cover her body

our madness contagious
desire shivers through me
I transform to couple

once swan   bull   satyr
eagle
now raven-black stallion

oh   joyous derangement
galloping from darkness
into blinding light

bonds broken she is
wild contentment
happiness   ecstasy

Robbery at the Musée Magritte

The day started as innocent
                as white roses. Brussels cloudy,
    cold. Magritte beckoning with his

cloth-covered faces, a pipe that
                is a pipe that he said wasn't.
    In two short hours, he had robbed us

of Reality, called it
                a boulder floating in the sky,
    given it the face of a green apple.

And in the turmoil of mantle clocks and locomotives,
                blind women, ravens, empires of light,
    the sea, we lost ourselves and then

each other. When panic set in
                and we could barely breathe,
    our hearts inhaled and exhaled.

Separately, we searched
                labyrinthine galleries, as invisible
    to one another as Magritte's *Lovers*.

Beyondness

I've been living where words
leave the dictionary and knock
on my door. Thinking
they're neighbors,
I open to
cancer and stroke.
They lounge on the couch
put their feet on the chairs,
heat the kettle to hide
the fears that snake through the walls.

Nothing seems quite real,
yet reality holds me prisoner.
Here time is everything
and nothing—a steady tick
around an impassive face.

Though I long to leave,
turn the lock in the door,
escape from other words
they've invited in—anger
and responsibility—the road
to Before has disappeared.
Its words a language
I no longer speak.

When a Voice Was All I Had

Fantasy on Faust by Mariano Fortuny

I read Goethe's Faust to my husband, hoping
to summon him out of the deep sleep
of his induced coma, the images as fantastic

as Fortuny's painting—Mephistopheles
in his red suit and feathered hat,
cajoling Martha the Pimp in noir,

the owl of death hovering. I read
to bring him back from the land of myth,
to unveil the false rhapsody of Faust and Margarete,

to lead him through the thick forest of pneumonia.
In the painting, notes rise from scores scattered
on an Oriental carpet, the passionate Pujol

playing his *Gran fantasia sobre Fausto*.
Faust's bargain with Mephistopheles, a possible soul
for the taking. Though my husband claimed

Mephistopheles was the more tormented
of the two, neither is totally blameless
nor evil. Two artists listen intently

as Pujol's notes fill the room.
The way I listen to the repeated wheeze
and sigh, compression boots closing tight,

then opening full, like an accordion,
pulsing blood through my husband's body.
Not knowing what bargain he might have made,

I read to head him off before the gates
to the underworld open.

Buy That Red Dress

A woman needs a man like a fish needs a bicycle.
　　　　　　　　　　　　—Gloria Steinem

I need back rubs and morning hugs.
Goofiness and giggling.
Occasional candlelight kisses.
My man's warmth in the kitchen.

Why can't a fish need a bicycle?

I need the rocks and fossils
of his love, the stones he places
in my palm after field trips
to Maine, Colorado, Kentucky.

I need the scent of supermarket flowers
I didn't buy, the spiciness of
his homemade bolognese or his
Let me take you out for dinner?

For him to say, *Buy that red dress!*

To myself I say, *Fish, you need a bicycle.*
Don a helmet, brace your fins
on the handlebars. Use
your tail to pedal.

Who am I to deny myself
the soft murmur
of his breathing deep in the night?

In a French Café

My husband sits in profile, hat tied under his chin,
eyes squinted, a clenched-teeth smile worthy
of Clint Eastwood. If the café terrace
weren't in a French harbor and the drink
a large *café crème,* instead of whisky in a saloon,
if there weren't a hundred sailboat masts
tied to the piers, instead of horses hitched to a post,
I could imagine he's just stepped out of
"The Good, the Bad, and the Ugly."
Man of the Hour would suit him, looking
into the sun with intention, yet longing
for that elusive something after seven decades
that could have put his name in lights.

A Path Home

After the Storm by Istvan Farkas

There were so many black clouds,
so many storms. Not just hurricanes
and polar freezes. Life-threatening illness,
a court case. We wore fear
draped around our shoulders,
tucked under overcoats. Any misguided word
created despair or released boiling anger.

We stood back-to-back, unable to face
opposition. Unable to move backward
or forward. Unable to trudge the path
toward home, its white-washed comfort
questionable. Was the deep purple horizon
winter's sunset or sunrise? No matter.
We would wait for the clouds to lift,
for spring to deliver its dark green promise.

Aerie

After Hurricane Ike on the Gulf Coast

The sky falls silent as a sleeping child
after a shattering tantrum. Calm air
wraps us, a dawning guarantee,
assurance that this time
the storm has passed.
We sit amidst brittle shadows
of sycamore and oak, mounds
of green pecans, breathing
the new-found comfort of French roast,
wafting across the porch.
We soak in the stillness,
welcome the mockingbird's
tentative song, though
slightly off-key to our ears,
the walls of our lungs
still battered by winds.

Sunrise Walk in the Heights

Red breast puffed out,
the robin—my morning Pavarotti—
sings the sun into the sky,
his chirpy vibrato awakening
Italian operas once shared

with my husband, who calls
to say he ran away last night,
tried to make himself disappear.
As I have disappeared in a city
that bars visitors from hospitals.

Dreams leak into his reality.
Medicine increases.
The veil grows thinner.
I turn onto a boulevard
lined on one side with live oaks

and stumble over the grief
their thick, aging roots
have caused—sidewalks broken,
sharp inclines, perilous declines.
If I could, I would cross the street.

No Visitors Allowed

I hold your hand through the telephone.
Fiber optics strung through clotted mud

connect the hospital and you to home.
Long strands of glass thin as human hair

carry light and voice, but not the warmth
of your fingers, the sweet pressure of your hug.

Hugs once happened every day. The touch.
I began with love, a word abused,

overused, empty some will say. *Don't go away.*
Optics course through hospital walls.

I'm no ghost passing through concrete.
The human body hasn't mastered that feat.

My spirit slips through clotted mud and roots.
I hold your hand through the telephone.

A Dream to Pierce the Dark

I Ask Van Gogh's *Starry Night* to Forgive Me

I want the stars to stop their frantic pinwheeling
before one is impaled on the church steeple.

I want thoughts to stop swirling
through my mind like shrieking cicadas.

Let me rest undisturbed under the cypress trees
whose roots grow straight down,

never interfere with a grave,
never tickle the dead.

Nevermore Forever

Poe Returns to Boston by Steff Rocknak

Nevermore leaps from Poe's suitcase.
He, alas, no better master
of grief than I, who greets each morning
with *forever.* A single word
engraved on my mind's front door.
Like hazardous weather, it ghosts
my hours, pricks my eyes, allows the Raven's
deep-pitched *raw raw raw* to tear
into my spleen. For a moment, I thought
I'd cornered grief, wrapped it safely
in an old quilt, stuffed it into
a worn, brown suitcase. Now, it's burst out
again, wild wings batting the air,
dropping feathers, ruffled
memories. *Nevermore* a shadow
forever on the kitchen floor.

Grief Has Its Habits

Now that you're gone, morning is dark.
Bach's partitas invade your room.
A melancholy violin bowed
to hit the highest and lowest notes.
Staccatos that herald and mourn
as another empty day unfolds.

Friends say to wait until life unfolds.
Yet no brightness in the sky erases dark.
Sometimes I can do no more than mourn
and seek solace seated in your room.
My breath catches in the glissando of notes,
their sharp rise, dramatic fall, my head bowed.

Masks spread across your study wall, their faces bowed
toward shelves of books. Another chapter unfolds.
Bookmarks hold your place, cramped notes
I cannot decipher in the dark.
Does your spirit wander this seductive room?
How many years must I sit and mourn?

At a friend's deathbed, I witnessed the wife mourn.
I want to go home, he said, his head bowed.
I'll send a sign from beyond this earthly room.
No word from him has ever come as time unfolds.
Still, I want a dream from you to pierce the dark.
Your voice to rise above a violin's notes.

What could be revealed in music's notes?
I ask. *Is this the proper way to mourn?*
Through your window, dawn attacks the dark.
A squirrel scampers. A fig tree's limb is bowed.
Blue jays tumble from the nest. New life unfolds.
If only your laughter would echo in the room.

Grief plays hide-and-seek in your room.
I try to hide, escape these painful notes.
But Bach's music in its own bitter-sweet time unfolds.
The presence of your absence insists I mourn.
The plaintive strings so tightly bowed.
No brightness in the sky can yet erase the dark.

In the Land of Shadow Puppets

I snuff out the candle just as the gamelan gong
        sounds once, twice. A moment of silence.

The drums begin to beat. Shadows march
        out of my mind. Guided by bamboo sticks

fixed to hands and feet, exotic shapes scissor
        across a sheet bleached white by light. They poke

elongated noses into my foibles and fancies.
        My hours pondering *le mot juste*. Holding the violin

of my dead husband's hand. An embrace
        finds us dancing through the kitchen.

Who are these shades from another culture
        whose playfulness stirs a flurry of memories?

Let them know my name.
        Let them be spirits come to guide me.

Through the Keyhole

After Breakfast by Elin Danielson-Gambogi

The woman's cigarette turns to ash,
the frail balloon of her thoughts rising
with the smoke. If I could slip

through the keyhole, I would sit
in the chair abandoned by her
breakfast friend, sip from the glass

of cold coffee, put out the burning
cigarette on the tablecloth's edge.
Remnants of companionship.

It's Saturday morning, days
after my husband's death, and I gaze
with the woman down the long hours ahead.

Grateful for the company and a day
that may be as empty as the shells
of her soft-boiled eggs or an egg cup

I could fill to the brim. Widowhood
has surprised me, arrived unannounced.
I'm drawn to her youth, all that lies ahead—

Italy, the Italian artist-husband,
a painting life. And remind myself
of the richness of my own past. Still, I envy

the rebellion born in her bones,
the different melody painted on
this canvas. She's a woman at home

in her skin, as the French love to say. Like her,
I could make myself into a perfect song.

Tankas: All the Tomorrows

Matthew 7:14

Fall leaves blown and bagged.
Grass yellow, blooms spent. Nature's
season of widows.
Then, the fig tree sprouts lime green.
My love's ashes around its trunk.

..

My blue car idles
before wrought-iron gates, vines thick.
Passage narrow, strait
the gate that leads *unto life,*
and few there be who find it.*

..

In sleep, a ghostly
visitation reveals gold.
A notched key hidden
on a back porch nail, unlocks
an ardor once lost to death.

Widow's Diptych
or Now That My Husband's Gone

i.

My apologies to the displaced wildlife
for obliterating the wooden deck,
for taking away your comfy lairs. Dead
leaves. Tired dirt. Forgive me,
beetles, spiders, centipedes
scurrying for refuge.

My apologies to the pipes,
corroded by chemicals and time, decades
of iron-red water lingering
in your passageways. Forgive me
for pulling out your galvanized hearts,
implanting PEX plastic.

To the snails who have nibbled holes
in the roof's shingles, I apologize.
How could you have known your feasts and
summer picnics wouldn't last forever.
Forgive me for having you scraped and scrapped.

And to you, venerable water heater
who served for 28 years, forgive me
for having you carted off
for a younger model. Forgive me house
in my search for new beginnings
as we age together, just the two of us now.

ii.

The clock strikes 4:30 a.m.
I sit at the window, staring
into darkness, dawn still far away.
A bird begins to sing. But
no chorus answers. There is only
this dark solo that might be grief,
to match my own, or a soliloquy
to the day's possibilities.
If this were Shakespeare, I would expect
Romeo and Juliet's chagrin.
Hark! Hark! The lark!
But such deadlines no longer
govern me. Love has come
and lived a few years in this house.
Now there's me and this bird
I cannot name. His trills,
his unexpected song.

This Is a Valentine

For the three tins of anchovies
        stacked in the pantry, wild-caught and preserved
                in olive oil and salt,
        to be used in the recipe you forgot to share.

For your desk drawer
        with myriad supplies carefully ordered.
                Paperclips and red pens, thick and thin
        rubber bands, Post-It notes I raid from time to time.

For the pineapple cubes
        in the back of the fridge I will never eat,
                the blue cheese dressing you liked,
        though you'll never arrive for dinner.

For your glasses and book
        on the bedside table, the oximeter, loyal gauge
                of the oxygen in your blood, instructions
        for the humidifier, its lulling white noise at night.

The old rocking horse in the shed,
        paint peeling from its once-black mane,
                the small remnant
        of your motherless childhood.

Your three pairs of shoes
        at the back door, your flat-footed struggle to wear
                the hiking boots and tennis shoes,
        for the final comfort of L.L. Bean moccasins.

The Pier One napkins,
    your Oneida ware, the dining room table where
        I finally sit again, book propped against
  the pewter of your candlestick.

The red candles
    I've yet to light like we did every night of our
        married life. For their soft glow
  to grace the table once again.

A Glass of Muscadet

I step through customs into
        anonymity. Train to Gare du Nord,
                taxi. My Paris hotel, where I nestle into

the skin of its narrow street. The grocer,
        the baker, the rows of curtained lives housed
                under chimney pots and garrets. A lone

song thrush, I perch on the windowsill,
        humming *No Regrets*. I still miss him,
                how we mused on Parisian street life—

the assembly line of passers-by, their lives
        and jobs. With him gone, my eyes turn skyward
                across the quiet white of mansard roofs.

Morning's soft rain pocks the night's snow.
        My thoughts drift to the solitary slice
                of yesterday. Apple tart at Le Fregate,

a glass of Muscadet, traffic slushing
        beside the winter-dark Seine. We once shared
                dinner here—a window table—drinking

in the city of light. Now only
        my passport knows my name. Sirens and horns
                fill the air. Smoke wavers above closed shutters.

Psyche Has a Word with the Poet

Cross My Heart by Caroline Bacher

Don't ignore the pliant hands, marble white,
the sculpted fingernails, the needle.
Don't bargain with time. Concentrate

on the eye painted in the hand's left palm.
Eye of the beloved, like a Georgian
"lover's eye." Remember when he held

the precious marble of your hand,
uncurled your fingers. Hear his gravelly voice,
"This is how I'll always see you."

Look at the woman's single eye
blue as a periwinkle, staring back
from a small oval broach. Feel his hand

wind a cherry-red ribbon around
your wrist. Remember the smile that twinkled
in his eyes, their hazel hue, warm

and full of life. Beware sharp objects—
those *if onlys*. Don't let them prick holes
in memory. Don't let them tear apart

your heart. Replay the embrace of that
first dance in your apartment, Michel Legrand
on the stereo playing "His Eyes, Her Eyes."

In a Galaxy Not Far Away

Gone our walks past the art school.
Gone its glass-block wall. Gone
my walking partner, our flickering

shadows. Rush-hour reflections
no longer waver in the glass
like supernovas—white headlights,

red taillights. Gone the blue-green night
of downtown's encroaching
darkness. Demolition, another

kind of death. But isn't that the way
of the universe? I enter an earthly space
of timeless symbols as cinematic

as photos sent back from outer,
or is that inner, space
where the gas and dust of a nebula

can be either the explosion of a dying
star or where new stars begin.
Each glass square once witnessed

a story. The first time we touched
hands, a shooting star. The first time
we kissed, a pulsar in the sultry heat

of a Southern summer. Now my walking
partner no longer orbits my life.
He has entered another dimension,

translucent as these glass blocks,
in another galaxy not far away.

Prescription for Widowhood

For Nancy

Fly to Santa Fe. Find Venus in the sky of a waxing moon. Give up maps and being *one who must know*. Your pathway is under construction in this city of red and green chiles, clanging cathedral bells, clay pots. Meditate when melatonin and the generous shaker of margaritas don't erase the loss of your beloved.

Hold a pot in your hands. Caress its earthy roundness, its circle of life and love. Be with it. It came out of fire, strong, alive. It deserves respect. Recognize the stories of its people, separated, displaced, broken as you have been.

Place your ear on the mouth of the pot. It once held water, grey grains of salt, essences of a pueblo. It will whisper stories about the four phases of life in languages ancient as its gods. Gather the words in Tiwa, Tewa, Towa, Diné. Your heart will understand each one.

When the winter solstice comes, ground yourself in clay. Bless your cracks, your breaks, your knocks, your rough edges. Sing into yourself. Hear a song of endurance singing back.

About the Author

Sandi Stromberg lives in Houston, Texas, after spending more than 20 years in Europe as a freelance writer, contributing editor, translator, and columnist. During that time, she published travel pieces, human interest stories, the ups and downs of raising and moving a family from country to country, and she reported on advances in the construction and crane industries from Finland to Italy. She remains an ardent lover of art, music, food, travel, and languages.

On arrival in Houston, she worked at the Jung Center, then was executive director of Brigid's Place, developing programming around feminine creativity and the feminine divine. From there, she returned to her love of writing. As an award-winning magazine feature writer and editor at the University of Texas MD Anderson Cancer Center, she edited and wrote for the institution's high-profile magazine, *Conquest* and its *Annual Report*. For four years in a row, 2010–2013, she was named Public Relations Communicator of the Year in the Lone Star Awards.

She came to poetry originally as a translator, Dutch to English, while living in the Netherlands and only began writing her own poems after moving to Houston. Since then, she has received several awards, been nominated three times for a Pushcart Prize, twice for Best of the Net, been a juried poet in the Houston Poetry Fest eleven times, and received a Fantastic Ekphrastic Award from *The Ekphrastic Review*—whose editorial staff she has recently joined.

She served as guest editor of *Untameable City: Poems on the Nature of Houston* and co-edited *Echoes of the Cordillera,* ekphrastic poems in response to the photography of Jim Bones.

Her work has appeared in many literary journals and anthologies (see Acknowledgments). Additional information is available at:
www.facebook.com/sandi.stromberg
or www.instagram.com/sandistromberg

She has been a member of The Authors Guild for thirty-three years. For ten years, she served on the board of Mutabilis Press, a poetry press dedicated to publishing poets living in Texas and the surrounding states. For twenty years, she facilitated popular writing classes, "Writing a Woman's Life," at the Jung Center in Houston, at Brigid's Place, and at the International Women's Writing Guild (IWWG) Summer Conference in Saratoga Springs, New York. She also led journaling classes for patients and nurses at MD Anderson Cancer Center.

She has two sons, two daughters-in-law, and two grandsons. One threesome lives in France and the other in Singapore. Her beloved husband, Bill Turner, died in 2021. His presence nourished her poetry for 25 precious years.

www.ingramcontent.com/pod-product-compliance
Lightning Source LLC
Chambersburg PA
CBHW070937160426
43193CB00011B/1712